THE
COLOSSEUM

Peter Chrisp

WAYLAND

GREAT BUILDINGS

THE COLOSSEUM

THE EMPIRE STATE BUILDING

THE GREAT PYRAMID

THE HOUSES OF PARLIAMENT

THE PARTHENON

THE TAJ MAHAL

Produced for Wayland (Publishers) Limited by
The Creative Publishing Company
Unit 3, 37 Watling Street, Leintwardine
Shropshire SY7 OLW, England

Series designers: Ian Winton and Sally Boothroyd
Book designer: Sally Boothroyd
Editor: Sabrina Crewe
Illustrations: Francis Phillipps and Clive Spong
Map: Peter Bull

First published in 1997 by
Wayland (Publishers) Limited
61 Western Road, Hove
East Sussex BN3 1JD, England

British Library Cataloguing in Publication Data
Chrisp, Peter
The Colosseum: how it was built and how it was used. –
(Great buildings)
1.Colosseum (Rome, Italy) – Juvenile literature
I.Title
725.8'27'09376

ISBN 0 7502 1989 0

Printed and bound in Italy by G. Canale & C.S.p.A., Turin

CONTENTS

IN THE ARENA

Two men faced each other under the blazing sun. They were in the arena, the sand-covered fighting area, of a huge open-air building called an amphitheatre. As the two circled each other, the shouts of 50,000 spectators echoed around the walls.

The hoplomachus carried a shield and sword, and was protected by a helmet and armour. The retiarius, or net-man, had only a leather guard on his left arm; his weapons were a trident and a net. The hoplomachus was better protected, but his armour slowed him down. The retiarius was easier to wound, but he was fast on his feet.

▲ This Roman vase is decorated with an image of a gladiator contest. The gladiator on the right has lost the fight, and is raising his finger to beg for mercy.

Suddenly, the retiarius threw his net. The hoplomachus jumped aside, but lost his balance. The retiarius closed in quickly, jabbing at his enemy. The hoplomachus' weapons dropped on to the sand. He held a finger up in the air, asking for mercy. Some of the crowd shouted, 'Finish him off!' Others stuck their thumbs in the air, yelling, 'Spare him! He fought bravely!' The final decision belonged to the Roman emperor, sitting in the front row. The fighters looked up at him, waiting to see what he would decide.

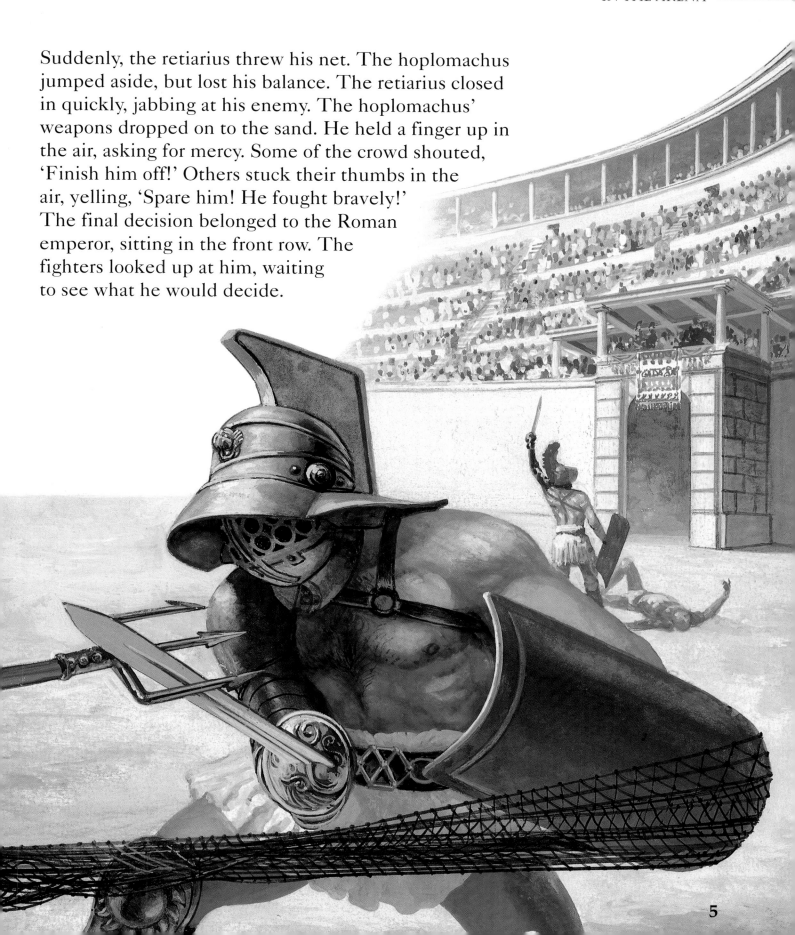

CHAPTER ONE

ROME AND THE ROMAN EMPIRE

▼ In the second century AD, the Roman Empire was at its height, and included all the lands around the Mediterranean Sea. Between fifty and ninety million people – about one fifth of the world's population at the time – lived under Roman rule.

The gladiators' contest took place two thousand years ago in the city of Rome. The Romans were rulers of a vast empire, made up of many countries. They had built up their empire thanks to their skill at battle. Once the soldiers had conquered a new land, the Roman government officials and tax collectors would arrive, together with builders, traders and craftspeople. Everything that the Romans did was well organized, from fighting wars to ruling over the conquered peoples.

◀ Every five years, all Roman citizens were registered by officials called censors, who kept details of people's names and wealth. This relief shows citizens being registered at a sacrificial ceremony.

▼ Slaves were treated as property, like horses or cattle. They could be bought and sold, and killed if their owners wished. However this slave carrying a tray of food was included in a floor mosaic, which even shows his name.

Throughout the empire, people came to share the Roman way of life. In places as far apart as Britain in the north-west and Egypt in the south-east, people dressed in similar clothes and worshipped the same Roman gods. They did their shopping with Roman coins and ate their meals from Roman pottery. People spoke one of two languages: in the western countries it was Latin, and in the east it was Greek.

Within the empire, there were different groups of people with different rights. At the top were the Roman citizens. In the first century AD, there were around six million of them. Far more people made up the second class of non-citizens. Right at the bottom were the slaves, people with no rights at all.

▶ The Romans were wonderful builders. Wherever they went, they built towns linked by long, straight roads. The Via Colosseo in Rome is still used today by visitors to the Colosseum.

Rome, the capital of the empire, was an enormous place. In the first century AD, more than a million people lived there. There were fashionable areas, where the rich lived in great mansions. There were also slum districts, where the poor people lived, crowded into tall blocks of cheaply-built flats.

The centre of the city was filled with grand public buildings. There were temples to the various gods, such as Vesta and Jupiter, who were believed to protect the city and the empire. There were also enormous bath houses, where people went to relax in the afternoons.

▼ This nineteenth-century drawing shows the centre of Rome as it was in AD270. The Colosseum (1) is in the centre of the background with the Forum (2) to its left. You can see the huge Stadium of Domitian (3) that was used for chariot races, and the Circus Maximus (4) that could hold 250,000 people.

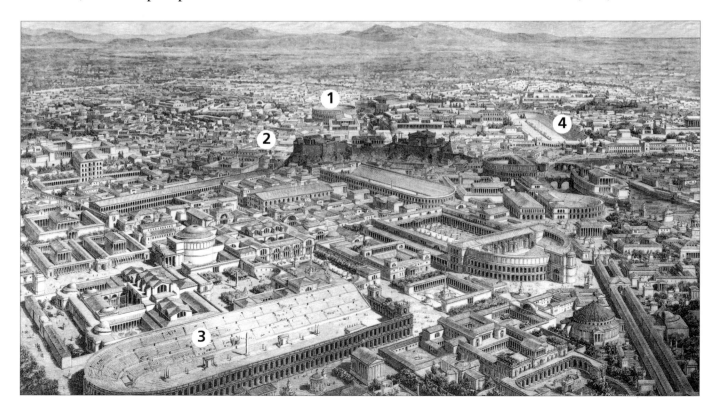

The biggest buildings of all were those used for public entertainment. The huge amphitheatre, the Colosseum, right in the centre of the city, was the tallest building in Rome. The Romans were proud of their city. It was described by one writer, Seneca, as 'the greatest and loveliest city in the world'.

▼ The Forum was at the centre of daily life for Romans. It was a meeting place and a market, and included temples and government buildings. You can see the Colosseum rising up behind the Forum ruins.

▼ Chariot races, held in huge stadia called circuses, were tremendously popular with the Romans. Here a four-horse chariot is approaching the three columns of the turning post. Just going around the post on horseback is the Jubilator, whose job it is to encourage the contestants.

The people of Rome were provided with a continual round of entertainment such as chariot races, plays and musical performances. Between one hundred and two hundred days of the year were public holidays, when the emperor put on free shows for the people.

The holidays were mainly religious festivals in honour of particular gods. There were also special shows to mark important events, such as a victory in war. The processions that formed part of these celebrations were great entertainments in themselves, with soldiers, musicians and slaves carrying religious statues, followed by animals to be sacrificed to the gods.

Almost every large Roman town had an amphitheatre, a place to see gladiators fighting. Fights between gladiators had started with the custom of killing prisoners of war or slaves at the funerals of rich Romans. This was a sacrifice to the spirit of the dead man. Later, slaves were forced to fight each other to the death at funerals. People enjoyed watching the fights, and they turned eventually into a form of entertainment.

Roman citizens expected their emperor and nobles to provide them with these free amusements. The emperor was also expected to provide free food, particularly wheat, which was distributed every month. The shows and the food were both needed to keep the thousands of poorer citizens happy and out of trouble. If an emperor failed to come up with either, there would be riots.

▲ Some Roman amphitheatres, such as this one at Arles in France, are still used today. If you look closely, you can see that the audience is watching a bullfight.

'The Roman people is held together by two things above all others – its food supplies and its shows.'

Fronto, a Roman writer

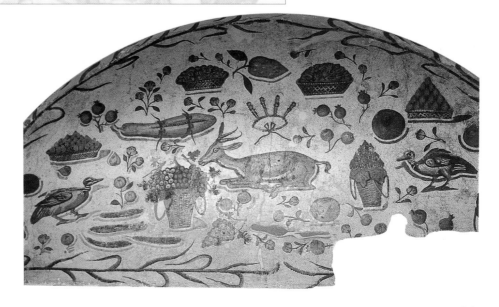

► The dishes prepared for a Roman banquet to celebrate a religious festival or an important event. The mosaic shows a gazelle in the centre, surrounded by vegetables, fruit and fowl.

CHAPTER TWO

THE PLAN FOR THE COLOSSEUM

In AD64, a terrible fire ripped its way through the heart of Rome. It burned for nine days before it was finally put out. When the Emperor Nero set about rebuilding the city, he saved a huge area right in the centre for a new palace. In the entrance of the Golden House, as Nero called his palace, there was a colossus, or gigantic statue, of the emperor himself. It was 37 metres high and made of shining bronze. Outside, Nero had a private park with a lake.

This bust is of Nero, who was the Roman emperor from AD54 to AD68, succeeding his stepfather Claudius when he was only seventeen years old. He went on to become one of the cruellest emperors, killing mercilessly and ruling with tyranny. Nero plundered the Roman Empire to pay for his extravagances, and was widely disliked.

The Golden House was hated by the people of Rome. At night, they wrote rude comments about their emperor and his palace on the walls of the city: 'The palace is spreading and swallowing Rome!' Nero was already unpopular with many Romans. He was known to have murdered his mother, his wife and his step-brother. Now, when people saw how well he had done out of the fire, many wondered whether he had started the blaze himself.

Nero had barely moved into his new home when he learned of widespread uprisings against his rule. The generals commanding Rome's greatest armies refused to obey Nero's orders, saying that they would make better emperors themselves. Abandoned by everyone, Nero killed himself.

▲ Inside the Golden House, the rooms were richly decorated. The dining rooms had ceilings of carved ivory with sliding panels to allow flowers or perfume to be showered down on the guests. This is one of the few surviving rooms, where the decorations are still faintly visible.

AD69—the year of many emperors
Nero's death was followed by eighteen months of war as rival generals fought each other for power. One after another, three men became emperor in Rome, only to be overthrown and die in their turn. Their portraits are stamped on these Roman coins: Galba (left), Otho (middle) and Vitellius (right). Whenever possible, Roman emperors used coins to celebrate their own heroism and importance.

By the end of AD69, there was a new emperor, an old general called Vespasian. In the previous eighteen months, four Roman emperors had died. Vespasian did not want to to be the fifth dead emperor. For his own safety, he needed to be popular with the people of Rome.

Vespasian decided to pull down most of Nero's hated Golden House and to open the grounds as a public garden. He also planned to build something for the people on the site. A huge amphitheatre for public shows would let everybody know that he was not going to be a selfish ruler like Nero. An amphitheatre, a place for the people, made a wonderful contrast with Nero's private pleasure palace.

▶ The Emperor Vespasian, who ruled the Roman Empire from AD69 until his death in AD79, the year before the Colosseum was opened. Two of his sons became emperor after him: first Titus (AD79-81) and then Domitian (AD81-96).

Vespasian died before the building was completed. It was opened in AD80 by his son, the Emperor Titus. The Romans called their new amphitheatre the Flavian Amphitheatre, after the family name of Vespasian and Titus. The later name Colosseum comes from the colossus, the gigantic statue of Nero which stood next to it. This was such an impressive statue that it had not been destroyed by Vespasian, just renamed as a statue of the sun-god.

▲ This relief from the Arch of Titus in Rome shows the Emperor Titus in a procession after the Romans destroyed Jerusalem. Spoils from the temple of Jerusalem are carried in triumph.

'Here, where the hated halls of a cruel king lately glistened, and one single house began to take over the whole city.... Here, where Nero had his fish ponds, the vast body of the magnificent amphitheatre now rises.... Rome has been given back to herself.'

Martial, a Roman poet

15

CHAPTER THREE

BUILDING THE COLOSSEUM

Although amphitheatres had been built before, no-one had ever built one as big as the Colosseum. The Emperor Vespasian wanted a building which could hold 50,000 spectators. The first step was to have a plan drawn up by an architect.

How would the architect make something big enough to hold all the people? It would have to be tall rather than wide, so that everyone would be close enough to see the gladiators. The problem with a tall building is that the weight of all the seating pushes outwards. So the outer walls had to be strong, to stop the building collapsing.

Another problem was one of crowd control. How do you get 50,000 excited people safely into and out of an amphitheatre? The answer was to have seventy-six different entrances, each with its own stairway to a seating area.

▼ The plan of the Colosseum (below) shows the overall shape as if you were looking down on it. The plan also shows entrances, columns and tiers. The cross-section (right) shows a slice of the building looking from the side.

16

A Roman architect had to have many different skills. As well as designing the building, he was in charge of construction. He was like a general in charge of an army. There were hundreds of workers and materials to organize and supply. Each of the materials used – brick, concrete, limestone, marble, wood and iron – was the speciality of a particular group of skilled craftsmen. There were also hundreds of unskilled workers, mostly slaves, to carry loads.

▲ This photograph taken from an aeroplane clearly shows the oval shape of the Colosseum. You can imagine how it would feel to be sitting high up in the amphitheatre, looking down on the contest below.

Guilds

The craftsmen who built the Colosseum would have been members of a guild, which is a group of people all practising the same craft. Stone cutters, bronzeworkers, brickmakers and bricklayers, concrete makers and carpenters – all would have worked on the Colosseum and all would have had their own guild. This stone carving shows a smith beating metal on his anvil.

▼ A modern-day marble quarry in Italy. White marble is the most beautiful and expensive building stone. The Romans used it for its decorative qualities, to build the lower seating and to line the inside walls of the Colosseum.

The Colosseum needed deep foundations to provide a firm base for its high walls. The architects had the clever idea of draining the lake of Nero's Golden House to use as the site of the amphitheatre. This was much easier than digging the foundations from scratch. So Nero's lake was emptied and a vast oval ring of concrete was poured in – 51 metres wide and 12 metres deep.

While the concrete workers were making the foundations, another workforce was busy 17 kilometres to the north-east of Rome. They were the stoneworkers, and it was

Concrete

Concrete was invented by the Romans, It was cheap, quick to make, and easy to use. To make concrete, the Romans dropped pieces of rubble into sticky mortar, made of lime (a powder of burnt chalk or limestone), water and pozzolana (a volcanic ash). The mortar hardened as it dried, holding the concrete together. Rubble gives concrete its strength. Big lumps of heavy rubble were used in the Colosseum's foundations. Small lumps of light rubble were used in the upper walls.

their job to cut the limestone blocks at the quarries. It was back-breaking work. There were no machines or explosives, and every block had to be cut by hand. The stoneworkers' main tool was a saw with no teeth. Sand was poured beneath the saw's blade, and the stone was slowly ground away.

The stone was taken to Rome on carts pulled by oxen. It has been estimated that 292,000 cartloads of stone were needed for the Colosseum.

▲ A road had to be specially built for transporting stone from the quarries to Rome. This model shows a Roman surveyor using an instrument called a groma to plot a straight road.

1. Scaffolding
2. Seating
3. Arch
4. Corinthian column
5. Walkway
6. Statue
7. Ionic column
8. Doric column
9. Crane with treadwheel
10. Underground passage
11. Cart with stone

◀ It took hundreds of workers eight years to build the Colosseum. This picture shows several different stages of its construction.

Stone was used on the outside walls and the sections of the building which took the most weight. Huge lifting cranes hoisted stone blocks into the air. They were powered by slaves walking round and round in a treadwheel. Inside walls and underground passages were built using heavy concrete and brick. The upper levels were built with less heavy materials, such as wood, bricks and the lightest concrete.

The outside walls were decorated with Greek columns; a different sort of column was used on each of the three lower levels. Between the columns were statues of gods and heroes, placed beneath the arches around the outside walls. On the topmost level, large bronze shields were hung, reminding people that this building was a place for combat.

The Colosseum was opened in AD80 by the Emperor Titus, with a hundred days of games. Building work continued on the top levels for a few years. The uppermost tier of columns was added by Titus' brother Domitian two years later, when he had become emperor. The completed building, at 57 metres high, towered over the centre of the city.

Arches and vaults

Arches were one of the main features of Roman architecture. They were built over a wooden frame that supported the stones or bricks until they were all in place. A vault is an extended arch built to form a passage or room. This arched walkway goes around the Colosseum on the first floor.

CHAPTER FOUR

▼ Early on the morning of a show, crowds of Romans entered the Colosseum. Seventy-six entrances and many numbered sections made it possible for people to find their way quickly to their seats.

THE GREAT SHOW

There was great excitement before a show in the Colosseum. The events were advertised with colourful signs painted on the walls, describing the attractions and listing the names of the starring gladiators. Heralds walked through the streets shouting announcements.

The show often began at dawn with music from an orchestra. The Romans were early risers. From all corners of Rome, 50,000 people made their way to the Colosseum. Entrance to the show was free, like all Roman entertainments, but only those who had been given tickets were allowed in. These ivory tokens, called tesserae, were carved with the numbers of their seat, row and section.

◄ This mosaic from a Roman villa in Germany shows musicians playing in an amphitheatre to entertain the audience.

Seating was arranged according to class. The emperor sat with his family in a marble box in the front row. Also in the front row were the most important people, such as senators and priestesses. Just above were lesser nobles and other wealthy citizens. The ordinary male citizens sat in the second tier; the third tier, hidden from below by a wall, was for women only. Right at the top, there was standing room for non-citizens, slaves and foreign visitors to the city

Togas
Romans wore their smartest clothes for a show at the Colosseum. For male citizens this meant putting on a toga, a woollen robe made from an oval piece of cloth about three times as long as the wearer was tall. It was arranged in complicated folds and draped around the body. Senators and important noblemen, such as this Consul, wore white togas with a broad purple stripe. Equestrians had a narrow purple stripe on theirs, while ordinary citizens wore plain togas.

Keeping cool
As the sun rose in the sky, the audience were protected by the huge linen velarium, or shade, which hung from poles on the topmost level. It was managed by a team of sailors, chosen for their skill in handling sails and ropes. They shifted it to follow the movement of the sun, so that the crowd was always shaded while the arena was brightly lit.

The opening events were light-hearted, designed to warm up the audience. There were fights between old gladiators armed with dummy weapons. Women also sometimes fought in the mornings using wooden swords, though some Romans found this shocking.

Morning was also the time for tricks by performing animals. Lions caught hares in their mouths and then released the creatures without hurting them. Elephants danced, juggled, wrote letters in the sand with their trunks, and even walked the tightrope. Pliny the Elder, a Roman writer, was amazed at the behaviour of one elephant: 'It is a known fact that one elephant, somewhat slow in learning its tricks, was often beaten with a lash by its trainer. In the middle of the night, this elephant was found to be practising its lessons!'

As the different events were taking place, the amphitheatre staff were busy shifting scenery and

▶ This stone carving from the British Museum shows two women gladiators fighting in a Roman amphitheatre in Greece. Female gladiators were outlawed in AD200 because of public disapproval.

animals. The floor of the arena was made of movable wooden sections over the labyrinth of passages and rooms below. Stage sets and cages containing animals could be hoisted up with pulleys directly into the sand-covered arena.

The emperor was part of the entertainment. Every now and then, he would stand up and throw coloured balls into the crowd. People who caught these could exchange them for prizes, such as baskets of food or gold coins.

'He urged the audience to enjoy themselves, calling them all "my lords", and cracking stupid and far-fetched jokes.'

The historian Suetonius describing the Emperor Claudius at a show

▼ The remains of the underground passages and rooms of the Colosseum. This is where animals and prisoners spent their last hours before being brought up into the arena.

After watching the tightrope-walking elephants and the fights with dummy weapons, the audience was ready to see some real blood. It was time to bring the wild beasts out from their dark cages beneath the floor of the Colosseum.

The wild beasts took part in different types of entertainment. Fierce animals, such as bulls and rhinos, were made to fight each other. They also fought with the bestiarii, skilled animal fighters armed with spears or bows.

This was also the time for public executions. People found guilty of murder or robbery were tied to stakes mounted in carts, and wheeled by attendants towards angry lions and tigers. The attendants carried whips and burning torches, to protect themselves and to drive the animals towards the victims.

The animals themselves were often as terrified as the criminals. They had spent the night in a small dark cage and now suddenly found themselves in the bright sunlight, surrounded by thousands of shouting people. Some tried to get back into their cages.

This ivory carving
and the one opposite
show bestiarii, armed
only with spears,
fighting lions in
the arena.

26

There was an interval at midday, when many people went out to eat a light lunch. Those who stayed could watch criminals who were forced to kill each other with swords. The writer Seneca described the shouts of the crowd at lunchtime: '"Kill him! Flog him! Burn him! Why does he run at the other man's weapon in such a cowardly way? Why isn't he more keen on dying?" And whenever there's a break they shout, "Let's have some throats cut in the meantime, so that there's something happening!"'

▲ A beast hunt is staged in the amphitheatre to entertain the crowd. You can see the bestiarii attacking the leopards with their spears. The central figure is a herald, carrying a tray with moneybags for the victorious huntsmen.

Roman emperors needed vast numbers of animals for their shows. When the Colosseum opened in AD80, 5,000 beasts were killed on a single day. Twenty years later, the Emperor Trajan celebrated a victory by having 11,000 animals killed in the Colosseum.

The Romans hunted animals in every country they had conquered. Wild animals were much more common in Roman times than they are today. Much of Europe was still covered with forest, where wolves and bears lived. In North Africa and the Middle East, you could still find lions and leopards. Elephants were still found in North Africa. These animals, and many others, were brought from the forests to die in amphitheatres all over the empire.

Lands outside the empire also supplied animals. The rulers of India sent tigers and elephants as gifts to the

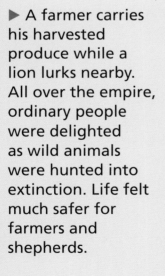

▶ A farmer carries his harvested produce while a lion lurks nearby. All over the empire, ordinary people were delighted as wild animals were hunted into extinction. Life felt much safer for farmers and shepherds.

Roman emperor. The people of Scotland caught bears and traded them with the Romans for luxury goods.

In time, the Roman hunts had a terrible effect on these animals. Elephants began to disappear from North Africa. Lions were wiped out in Mesopotamia (Iraq). It became more and more difficult to find wild beasts for the amphitheatres.

The animals were kept in a zoo by Rome's eastern gate. On the night before a show, they were driven into crates and taken by wagons to the Colosseum, where they were locked in the cages below the arena.

▲ The Romans became expert at hunting, transporting and looking after thousands of wild animals. The beasts were brought by road and by sea from all parts of the empire. This mosaic shows an antelope being led up a gangplank and on to the ship which will take him to Rome.

29

CHAPTER FIVE

THE GLADIATORS

In the middle of the afternoon, the part of the show that everyone had been waiting for was announced with a loud trumpet blast. Excitement grew as people realized that the gladiators would soon be fighting. They gambled money, betting on their favourites.

The gladiators walked in a procession into the arena, dressed in brightly coloured robes. They marched towards the emperor's box and greeted him, shouting, 'Hail Emperor, we who are about to die salute you!' Then the weapons were handed out. The men took off their robes and got ready to fight.

▶ This mosaic shows a victorious gladiator crouching next to his dead opponent. Next to the fighters is an umpire in a white tunic, who is acclaiming the winner.

Helmets and armour

Gladiators were armed in a variety of ways. The Thracian had a short curved sword and a tiny round shield. The hoplomachus held a straight sword and crouched behind a long curved shield. Some wore body armour designed to protect the gladiator from light wounds to his limbs which might stop him fighting. The chest, where an injury would kill, was usually unprotected. Myrmillo gladiators, who often fought the net-men, had bronze fish mounted on their huge helmets.

Both these helmets were worn by gladiators. Some helmets formed complete masks over the gladiators' faces.

The fight continued until one man was killed or asked for mercy. If his appeal was turned down by the emperor, he was expected to kneel on the ground and allow his throat to be cut without complaining.

Attendants dressed as underworld gods approached each fallen gladiator. One carried a red-hot iron to prod him, to make sure that he was not pretending to be dead. The other held a huge hammer to finish him off with. Once they were certain he was dead, they dragged his body out through the Gate of Libitina, goddess of death, to be stripped of its armour. The blood-stained sand was raked over, and the next fight could begin.

There were various ways of ending up as a gladiator. It was a punishment given to criminals and to slaves who had upset their owners. Foreign prisoners, captured in wars, were also sent to fight in the amphitheatre.

Sometimes, free men willingly became gladiators. Some were desperate, unable to think of any other way to live. They knew that they would be well fed, and they might only have to fight two or three times a year. Others simply liked fighting. Many gladiators won their freedom only to sign on again when they missed the excitement of the arena and the cheers of the crowds. When a free man became a gladiator, he had to swear a solemn oath that he would allow himself to be 'burnt by fire, chained, whipped with rods, and killed by the sword'. This meant that his trainer could do whatever he liked with him.

▼ This stone carving is part of a triumphal arch, celebrating Roman victory over the Gauls. Roman soldiers are holding captured weapons, and their prisoners can be seen below. Some of these foreign captives might have been sent to fight as gladiators.

The gladiators were housed in barracks next to the Colosseum. The barracks had a small arena for training which was surrounded by rooms for living in. Much of the gladiators' time was spent practising with wooden weapons. As well as learning to fight, gladiators were trained not to show fear or pain. Nothing was more disgraceful for a gladiator than to cry out if he was wounded.

Successful gladiators could earn a lot of money in prizes. They were treated like pop or film stars today.

▶ A bronze statue of a gladiator, one of the most popular subjects in Roman art. The rewards for a successful gladiator were fame and glory, but they paid a high price in surrendering their freedom, and often their lives.

'Celadus, glory of the girls, makes all the girls sigh.'

Graffiti about a celebrated retiarius, found at the Roman town of Pompeii

▲ The superstitious gladiators chose certain gods for particular worship. This silver statue shows Fortuna, goddess of good luck, who was their favourite. The gladiators also took stage names that they hoped would bring them luck, such as Victor (Winner) and Celadus (Applause).

33

Roman emperors were always looking for new ways to entertain the public. There was a danger that people would grow bored seeing the same animals being hunted, the same types of gladiator fighting, and criminals being killed in the same familiar ways.

One kind of show that always went down well was a mock sea battle. The Emperor Domitian decided to mount a sea battle inside the Colosseum itself. The floor of the arena was waterproofed with canvas. Water was piped in to flood the amphitheatre, deeply enough to carry full-size warships. The sight of ships floating inside the building was astonishing.

Mock sea battles were rarely put on because they were so expensive. They needed warships manned by thousands of gladiators. The aim was to re-enact a famous sea battle from history, such as one fought between the Greeks and the Persians. The gladiators who performed had to dress up as Greek and Persian warriors.

◀ This coin shows a Roman galley similar to the ones used in mock sea battles.

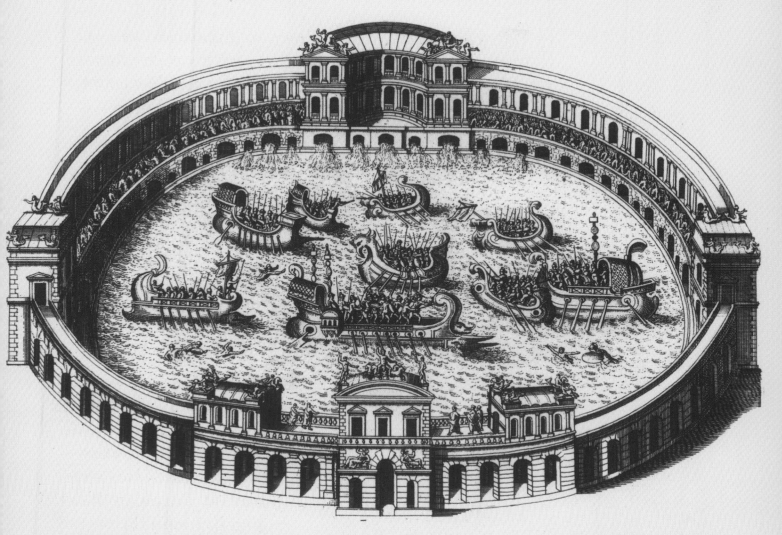

For the men forced to take part, there was nothing pretend about a mock sea battle. They fought to the death. The warships, powered by oarsmen, sped across the water, trying to ram and sink each other. Gladiators stood on deck, ready to leap on board a rival ship for hand-to-hand fighting.

In AD52, 19,000 gladiators took part in a sea battle staged by the Emperor Claudius. It was described by the historian Tacitus: 'There was energetic rowing, skilful steering, charging, and all the incidents of a sea battle. Though the fighters were criminals they fought like brave men. After much blood letting, the survivors were spared.'

▲ A seventeenth-century engraving showing the strange spectacle of an amphitheatre flooded for a battle. The arena was not really big enough for the warships to move around or build up speed. Mock sea battles in Rome usually took place on a lake, specially built for the purpose beside the River Tiber. The lake was three times the size of the Colosseum floor and much more effective.

Today people often find it hard to understand why the Romans enjoyed watching people killing each other. In many ways, the Romans were just like us. How could they have enjoyed the shows in the Colosseum?

Every Roman grew up surrounded by images of gladiators. Children played with gladiator dolls. Even babies' bottles had gladiators pictured on them for luck. The idea was that the baby would drink in the fighter's strength with the milk. People decorated their homes with pictures of gladiators fighting and criminals being torn apart by lions.

Most Romans saw nothing cruel or wrong in the games. They believed that it was a good thing to kill criminals and dangerous animals. It was also sensible to do it in public, to show everyone that crimes were punished. People in the audience found this reassuring. They didn't question whether it was right, but simply enjoyed the show, swept along by the exciting atmosphere.

◀ Reminders of gladiators were everywhere. Familiar household objects, like this Roman oil lamp, were carved with images of gladiators.

Some Romans were completely obsessed by the games and gladiators. The most famous was Commodus, who was emperor from AD180 to AD192. Although he was ruler of a vast empire, his real interest was in fighting as a gladiator. He appeared in the Colosseum as a wild beast fighter and as a secutor, fighting the net-men. He killed animals for practice in his palace, and had his own room in the gladiators' barracks next to the Colosseum.

The huge statue of the sun-god, which stood next to the Colosseum, was converted into a statue of Commodus. Inside the building, Commodus had the arena divided by walls topped with a platform, from which he could fire arrows at the animals from a safe distance. During one show, he killed a hundred bears from his platform. Sometimes he went down into the arena and killed tame animals, including tigers and elephants.

Roman emperors were not supposed to behave like this. Commodus' closest companions decided to kill him. On New Year's Eve, AD192, the gladiator-emperor was strangled while taking his bath.

▲ Commodus modelled himself on Hercules, the legendary strong man and hunter. This statue shows him in a lion's skin and carrying a club, just like Hercules.

'We senators always had to be there when the emperor (Commodus) was fighting. We would shout whatever we were told, and especially these words continually: "You are the lord and you are the best! You are the victor and always will be!"'

Dio Cassius, a Roman senator

▼ The Romans worshipped many different gods. When they conquered a country, they welcomed its gods into their own religion. They thought that the more gods you had on your side, the better. This beautiful mosaic shows Romans performing religious rites to the gods of the River Nile in Egypt.

CHAPTER SIX

THE END OF THE GAMES

Around the year AD107, a man called Ignatius was on his way from Syria to Rome. He had been arrested for being a Christian, a follower of the new religion which was spreading throughout the Roman Empire at the time. The Christians were the first to speak out against the cruelty and killing of the games. It was against the law to be a Christian, and the punishment was death.

◄ This nineteenth-century engraving shows Ignatius as he was thrown to the lions in the Colosseum.

Ignatius was being taken to Rome to be fed to the lions in the Colosseum. Unlike most people in this situation, Ignatius was happy. He wrote: 'How I look forward to the lions that have been got ready for me!... I shall encourage them to eat me quickly.... If they refuse, I will force them to do it...splintering of bone and mangling of limb...let every horrid and devilish torture come upon me, if only I may win my way to Jesus Christ!'

The Romans were usually happy to let people follow any religion that they wished to. The problem with the Christians was that they would only worship one god. They believed that all the Roman gods were devils and they would not pray or make offerings to them. The Romans worried that the Christians' behaviour would make the gods angry. The gods would punish everyone for the lack of respect shown by the Christians.

Christians were blamed for every disaster. A Christian writer called Tertullian wrote that if there was a famine or a plague, the cry was always, 'the Christians to the lions!' However, the Christians believed that by dying publicly for their beliefs they would go straight to heaven and encourage others to join them. So they stood in the arena, waving their arms to attract the wild beasts. This behaviour and strength of faith baffled the crowd watching the show.

Eusebius, a Christian writer, described the scene in the amphitheatre: 'Nothing could be more amazing than the fearless courage of these saints.... You would see a youngster not yet twenty standing without chains, spreading out his arms in the form of a cross, not budging in the least, though bears and panthers breathing fury and death almost touched his very flesh.'

▶ This stone carving of the Roman games shows a man, possibly a Christian, who has been thrown to the lions to be devoured.

Christians were killed for more than two hundred years by the Romans, but nothing could stop the spread of their religion. The turning point came in AD312, when Constantine became emperor. He was himself a Christian and he gave his fellow believers freedom of worship. No more Christians would be thrown to the lions.

This was not enough for the Christians, who wanted all killing in the amphitheatres stopped. In AD404, a monk called Telemachus jumped into the arena to try to stop a gladiatorial fight. A riot started and Telemachus was torn to pieces by the angry crowd. The Emperor Honorius used this as an excuse to ban all fights between gladiators. After three hundred years, the killing was over.

▲ A painting of the Emperor Constantine, known as Constantine the Great, with his mother Saint Helena. According to legend, Saint Helena discovered the cross on which Christ was crucified in the Holy Land, where she was founding churches.

41

CHAPTER SEVEN

AFTER THE GAMES

When gladiator fights were banned in AD404, the Roman Empire was already falling apart. Warlike German tribes were pouring over the borders and overpowering Rome's armies. By AD410, Rome itself had been captured.

Despite everything, life in Rome went on, and animal shows were still staged in the Colosseum. With the empire gone, it was much harder to find wild beasts. Instead farm animals, such as bulls and horses, were used. The last beast show was held in the year AD523.

▼ In the 1400s the Colosseum became a quarry – a wonderful source of stone and other building materials. Bits of the Colosseum are now spread all over Rome, in palaces, churches and walls built at the time.

Over time, the Colosseum has come to have a different meaning for different groups of people. In 1144 it was turned into a fortress by a Roman family. From the 1200s to the 1400s, the Colosseum was used at various times to stage religious plays. In the 1400s, there were bullfights in the arena. From the 1700s, Catholics came to see the Colosseum as a holy place, because of all the Christians who had died for their faith there. A cross was set up in the centre of the arena and Catholics went to pray there.

By the 1800s, the Colosseum had become completely overgrown. The botanist Richard Deakin found 420 different species of plants growing there. In the late 1800s, all the plants were removed by the Italians, who were restoring the ruin. They cleared away the earth and revealed the tunnels beneath the arena. The Colosseum became the tourist sight that we see today.

It is now more than 1,500 years since the last gladiators fought and died inside the walls of the Colosseum. Since then, it has been shaken by seven earthquakes and used as a quarry. Yet the amphitheatre still stands, reminding us of the power of the Emperor Vespasian who built it, and the thousands of people and animals who died within its walls.

'Never in its bloodiest prime can the sight of the gigantic Colosseum, full and running over with the lustiest life, have moved one heart, as it must move all who look upon it now, a ruin. God be thanked: a ruin!'

The writer Charles Dickens in *Pictures from Italy*, 1844

▼ The Colosseum survives today in the centre of the busy city of Rome. But the remaining stonework is being damaged by heavy pollution from traffic and industry.

TIMELINE

73-1BC	AD1-199	AD200-399	AD400-599	AD600-799

73-71 Unsuccessful uprising by slaves in southern Italy, led by the gladiator, Spartacus

29 First stone amphitheatre built in Rome

54-68 Rule of the Emperor Nero

64 Great fire in Rome

69 After eighteen months of civil war, Vespasian becomes emperor

72 Building of the Colosseum begins

80 Opening of the Colosseum

180-192 Rule of Commodus, who fights in the Colosseum as a gladiator

200 Women banned from fighting as gladiators

217 After being struck by lightning, the wooden floor of the amphitheatre catches fire

313 Emperor Constantine ends the killing of Christians in the amphitheatres

392 Worship of the old gods banned. Only Christianity is now allowed

404 Emperor Honorius bans gladiatorial games

410 Rome captured and plundered by the Goths, a German people

476 Last western emperor overthrown

523 Last animal games held in the Colosseum

600 Colosseum becomes overgrown

AD800-999 **AD1000-1199** **AD1200-1399** **AD1400-1599** **AD1600-1900**

800 Christians begin pilgrimages to Rome and visit Colosseum

1144 Colosseum becomes a military stronghold for a powerful Roman family

1263 Religious plays put on in the Colosseum

1332 Bullfights staged in the Colosseum

1450s Colosseum used as a quarry for building materials

1744 Memorial cross to martyred Christians erected in Colosseum

1871 Italians begin to restore the Colosseum

GLOSSARY

Amphitheatre
An oval building for public shows, especially gladiator and wild beast fights. The name means 'place for viewing from all sides'.

Arena
The fighting area inside an amphitheatre. The word itself means 'sand'.

Bestiarii
Beast-fighters: either skilled gladiators who fought wild animals, or criminals condemned to be eaten by them.

Equestrians
Men who belonged to the second most powerful class of Roman nobles.

Games
Free public shows, including chariot races, theatrical performances and gladiator fights.

Gladiator
Someone who fought in the amphitheatre.

Hoplomachus
A gladiator who had a long shield, a straight sword and wore some protective armour.

Secutor
'Pursuer' – a type of gladiator who fought against the net-men.

Thracian
A gladiator who carried a short curved sword and a small shield.

Retiarius
'Net-man' – a gladiator armed with a net and a trident (three-pronged fishing spear).

Senators
Men who belonged to the richest and most powerful class of Roman nobles. They acted as the emperor's advisers; they commanded armies; and they governed areas of the empire.

Velarium
Linen cloth fixed to masts to provide shelter from the sun for the crowd in an amphitheatre.

FURTHER INFORMATION

BOOKS

Joanne Jessop, David Salariya, *The X-Ray Picture Book of Big Buildings of the Ancient World*, Watts, 1992

Peter Connolly, *Pompeii*, Oxford University Press, 1990

Anthony Marks, Graham Tingay, *The Romans*, Usborne, 1990

Peter Chrisp, *Family Life in Roman Britain*, Wayland, 1994

Fiona Macdonald, *A Roman Colosseum*, Inside Story series, Macdonald Young Books, 1996

Richard Wood, *Architecture*, Legacies series, Wayland, 1994

VIDEOS

Stanley Kubrick, *Spartacus*, 1960

CD-ROMS

History of the World, Eyewitness series, Dorling Kindersley Multimedia, 1995

Romans!, Anglia Multimedia, 1996

Picture acknowledgements

The publishers would like to thank the following for allowing their pictures to be reproduced: Lesley and Roy Adkins: 7 (bottom), 23 (top), 32; Archivi Alinari: 37; Ancient Art & Architecture Collection: pages 7 (top), 11, 13 (bottom), 17 (bottom), 27 (left), 28, 30, 33 (right), 34, 36, 40; Bridgeman Art Library/Prado: page 42; British Museum: pages 24, 33 (left); Colchester Museums: page 4; C M Dixon Photo Resources: pages 19, 26, 27 (right); ET Archive: pages 12, 14, 38, 41; Mary Evans Picture Library: pages 8 (bottom), 39; Werner Forman Archive: pages 13 (top), 15; Sonia Halliday Photographs: pages 18, 29; Robert Harding Picture Library: page 11 (top); Michael Holford Photographs: pages 10, 23 (bottom); Angelo Hornak Photograph Library: page 8 (top), 21; Image Bank: front cover (Alan Becker); pages 17 (top), 22; Impact Photos: page 25; Mansell Collection: page 35; Tony Stone Images: pages 9, 43; Wayland Picture Library: pages 3, 31, 44-5.

INDEX